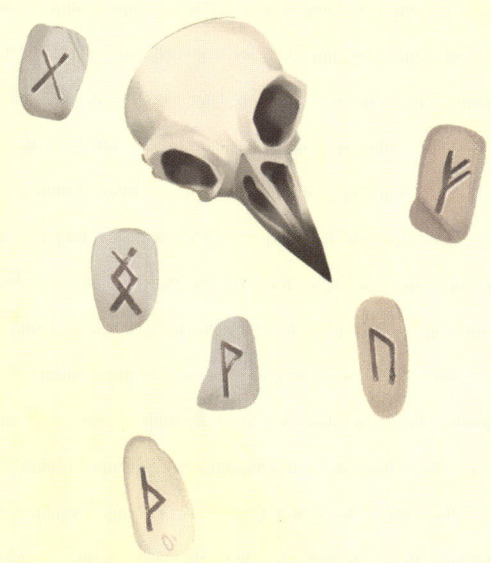

AVERY EVERYWHERE

A Day with the Vikings

Text by
Jacopo Olivieri

Illustrations by
Clarissa Corradin

This is Avery.
Avery Everywhere.

A strange nickname for a young boy, right?

But wait until you hear how he got it. Just by blinking his eyes, Avery is transported to another country...
AND ANOTHER TIME IN HISTORY!

Some say that he just has an overactive imagination.
Yet, if you believe Avery, everything he says really does happen to him!

For example, today he's Averik, a Viking boy from 890 CE!

A bit of Viking history

793 CE
The Viking era begins with the assault of the monastery of Lindisfarne, on the east coast of England.

825 CE
The Viking Naddodd discovers Iceland and colonizes it in the following years.

862 CE
According to legend, King Rurik conquers the Russian town of Novgorod. His descendants will go on to found the Kievan Rus', which will give Russia its name.

872 CE
Harald Fairhair defeats the king of Sweden and unites Norway under his kingdom.

890 CE
Our story begins here, in 890 CE, right in the middle of the Viking era.

911 CE
In return for protection, King Charles I of France agrees with the Viking monarch Rollo to give up the region that will take the name of Normandy. Rollo and his descendants and followers became the Normans.

982 CE
After beng banished from Iceland, Erik the Red sails to Greenland.

1016 CE
The Vikings raid London, and King Æthelred gives up his throne to the Viking king Cnut the Great, who reigns for nineteen years.

1030 CE
Thanks to the popularity of Christian king Olaf II, Christianity spreads to Norway.

1066 CE
The Viking era ends: England wins the Battle of Stamford Bridge, defeating the Vikings. In the same year, however, William (a Norman descendant of the Vikings!) conquers England.

Chapter 1

A VERY SPECIAL DAY...

Averik rubs his eyes. Usually his mom wakes him up, but today is a special day: His uncle is coming back! He bolts upright on his wooden bench and pushes away the soft animal furs that kept him warm during the night.

His dad has already left his bench; of course, he always wakes up before dawn to work in the fields. Averik gets up and yawns. In their *bœr*—the farm—there are several buildings, and the best one is definitely their house, which is one big, rectangular room. It is a bit dark because there are only some narrow openings that let the light in and keep the cold out. The walls are dark and slightly red-tinted; that's the color of the peat that has been cut into thick, compact bricks.

The roof is made of wood, covered with patches of grass that make it look like part of the fields that surround the farm.

Next to the house there is a building with the sauna and a stable. His mom is already at work by the large fireplace. Averik approaches—he loves the warmth coming from it!

That's not all; Mom is preparing the *dagverdhr*, and the smell of the soup makes his stomach rumble.

"Get your bowl and your spoon," his mom says to him.

Averik is starving and is about to attack his food when the door opens wide.

"So, are you ready?" inquires a cheerful voice, after having greeted his mom.

It's Astrid, being a pest as usual.

"What are you doing here?" Averik asks.

"We agreed...have you forgotten?" the girl asks, emphasizing the last words.

Right, now that he's reminded, Averik recalls that he told her to stop by early.

"Don't you dare make me late! Your uncle's ship must be at the harbor already!" she says. Then she gets close to him and, being careful not to be heard by his mom, she whispers into his ear, "Oh, I wish I could have been on that ship!"

Averik sighs. Astrid is always dreaming of going out to sea, but as a girl she's not allowed.

So, she confesses her desire only to him, with her quick way of talking that makes his head spin!

"There is no time to eat now!" she exclaims, dragging him to the door.

"Wait!" Mom says. "I need the spices for the *nåttverdhr* tonight. Get some at the harbor; there is always someone selling fresh ones. You can give this in exchange." She hands him a piece of colorful *vadhmal,* a very strong fabric.

Wonderful, now his day is complete.

"And remember that today I'm making an exception but tomorrow we will have to resume school," his mother shouts after him, while Astrid drags him away.

His uncle's ship must have arrived for sure!

> Don't get into trouble and don't forget about the **NÁTTVERDHR**!

What a family!

In Viking families like ours, all members depend on the *húsbóndi*, the head of the family, and on the *húsfreyja*, his wife and lady of the house, which is me!

However, I don't have the same rights as my husband. For example, **I can't speak during assemblies**, I can't be a judge in a trial, and I am not allowed to participate in politics.

I MUST BOW TO MY FATHER'S AUTHORITY, AND TO MY HUSBAND'S AS WELL, BUT I CAN FILE FOR DIVORCE.

THE QUEEN OF THE HOUSE

There is a place where I get lots of respect: **My house**!

And I'm very busy in there. I raise the children and look after their education, I take care of the elderly, I manage our finances and the family assets, I cook, and I keep everything tidy. I also hold the keys to wardrobes and the pantry: I always carry them with me, hanging from my belt. Only I can decide when to use them!

I also weave and embroider. I work in the fields, and I make butter and cheese.

IF I SEE THE POOR OR BEGGARS HANGING AROUND, I TRY TO LOOK AFTER THEM.

WHAT ARE WE EATING?

We Vikings usually wake up at six in the morning as there is always so much to do! In summer, we start working in the fields very early. Women prepare the *dagverdhr*, which is the most important and nutritious meal, and we eat it around **nine in the morning**. In the evening, around nine, we eat the *nåttverdhr*. During the day we sometimes recharge our energy with a third, lighter meal.

Among the most common foods we have are soups made with cereals, bread, and barley cakes, on which we spread butter and, if one likes, freshly cooked or dried fish, with dry algae and vegetables.
We also eat meat, often in delicious stews, and cheese (either soft or matured).
Our desserts and cakes are honey-based; we also enjoy fruit, such as berries and apples, and walnuts.

Food is ready!

We eat from wooden bowls, using spoons and knives (forks don't exist yet!).

Although only the rich use tablecloths, everybody enjoys gathering around large and robust wooden tables.

Men drink a lot of *öl*, our **beer** (we make several different types by fermenting the barley that we grow in our fields), and mead, a drink obtained by fermenting honey.

We drink from containers that are horn-shaped (made out of wood or metal), which we take turns passing from one person to another.

Chapter 2
WINTER IS COMING!

That cheeky Astrid! She dragged him out of the house, and now she's running as fast as the wind...soon he'll be unable to keep up with her! Averik speeds up. His jaws tighten as he pushes on, until a sudden cry pierces the silence. "Ouch!"

He slows down and almost tumbles over Astrid, who's tripped over something. Actually, someone!

"Gerd? What...?!" exclaims Averik, recognizing the farmer.

"This hurricane has swept me over!" he replies while getting up. Astrid's cheeks are bright red with embarrassment. "I'm sorry, we are so late that..."

"Well, you've hit me quite hard so now help me, OK?" says Gerd, frowning. "Actually we are..." Astrid begins to reply.

"Of course we are going to help you, as a way to apologize," Averik interrupts her. The three reach his stable. "Here we are," says Gerd. "Help me tidy up the hay that I've just harvested and now needs to dry...we will soon need it because winter is coming!"

Astrid and Averik look despairingly at the quantity of hay spread over the stable floor. It will take them the whole day! Noticing Astrid sulking, the farmer asks her, "Do you like dry meat?" She nods.

"Then you can give me a hand digging the holes where we preserve the meat during the wintery cold."

Astrid is speechless. "We will never see the end of this," she sighs.

"Well, how come you were in such a hurry before? Do you think that there is nothing to do here in the fields?" Gerd giggles, looking at the two children.

Averik suddenly gets it! Gerd is mocking them! He grabs his friend and drags her out of the stable. It's time to resume their trip. Who knows what his uncle is thinking at this moment; he must have gotten off the boat by now...

> Quick, quick! **WINTER** is coming!

SEASONS

For us Vikings there are two *misseri*, or seasons: summer and winter. We divide time based on **winters** and **nights**, counting the passing of winters (instead of the years) and of nights (instead of the days).

The year begins with the **cuckoo month** (around mid-April), when we **plow the fields** and take the animals outside after the long winter.

Summer lasts until mid-October; that's when the second misseri, **winter**, starts.

LET'S GO AND WORK...IN THE FIELDS

At the beginning of summer we sow **oats**, **rye**, and most importantly, **barley**.

We use barley flour to make **bread** and **barley cakes**. When we ferment the barley, we get **beer**. From the fields we also collect **peat**, which we form into the **bricks** to build our houses. We also use peat as **fuel** to keep warm.

BUT THERE'S MORE. WE FERTILIZE THE SOIL, AND WE CHOP WOOD AND REPAIR OUR BOATS AND EVERY OTHER THING THAT THE COLD HAS DAMAGED...
THERE'S NO TIME TO WASTE!

WITH THE SUN'S FAVOR...

During summer, we have many more tasks to do beyond looking after the fields. We collect **the eggs** of wild animals (very tasty but difficult to find!). We shear the sheep and take them to higher pastures (called **transhumance**), and we go hunting and fishing (the Baltic and the North Seas are very rich with fish!). What we don't eat right away is usually left to dry so that we can preserve it and consume it during the cold season.

In mid-June, the *sólmánadhr*, the month of the sun, starts. During this month, the *thing* (the assembly of free men) takes place.

THE THING IS SUMMONED TO DECIDE EVERY SINGLE ISSUE THAT IS IMPORTANT TO THE COMMUNITY.

There is always lots to discuss; we Vikings are famous for being overly sensitive!

The most serious offense is stealing (even more serious than murder!), and the punishment can be death, exile, the payment of a compensation sum, or sometimes the *holmgang* (a **duel**).

Summer is the period of the year when we **travel** by sea the most, in search of adventure and conquests! When winter comes, we never feel sad despite all those long, dark hours. Quite the opposite! We have parties and **invite guests,** so long as the weather allows it. We organize banquets with **dancing** and all sorts of entertainment…

THERE IS ALWAYS SOMETHING WORTH TOASTING TO!

Chapter 3
NOBODY IS ALLOWED TO INSULT THE CLAN!

The closer they get to the water, the lighter Astrid's mood becomes. Averik is excited too. The view at the harbor is spectacular! The steep sides of the mountains drop sharply into the sea. The luscious green of the grass blends into the blue of the sky and of the water to form beautiful color variations. And then, there they are: the ships! There are so many people around; many boats must have come back.

"Hey, Liv!" Astrid shouts, waving her arms to be seen through the thick crowd of muscular Vikings. Averik's eyes follow his friend, and he sees a girl approaching. But she's not alone!

With her is a man with a light, braided beard and dark eyes. His long cloak is huge and black, and it covers him almost completely. The sight sends a shiver down Averik's spine. "You're here too!" Astrid says.

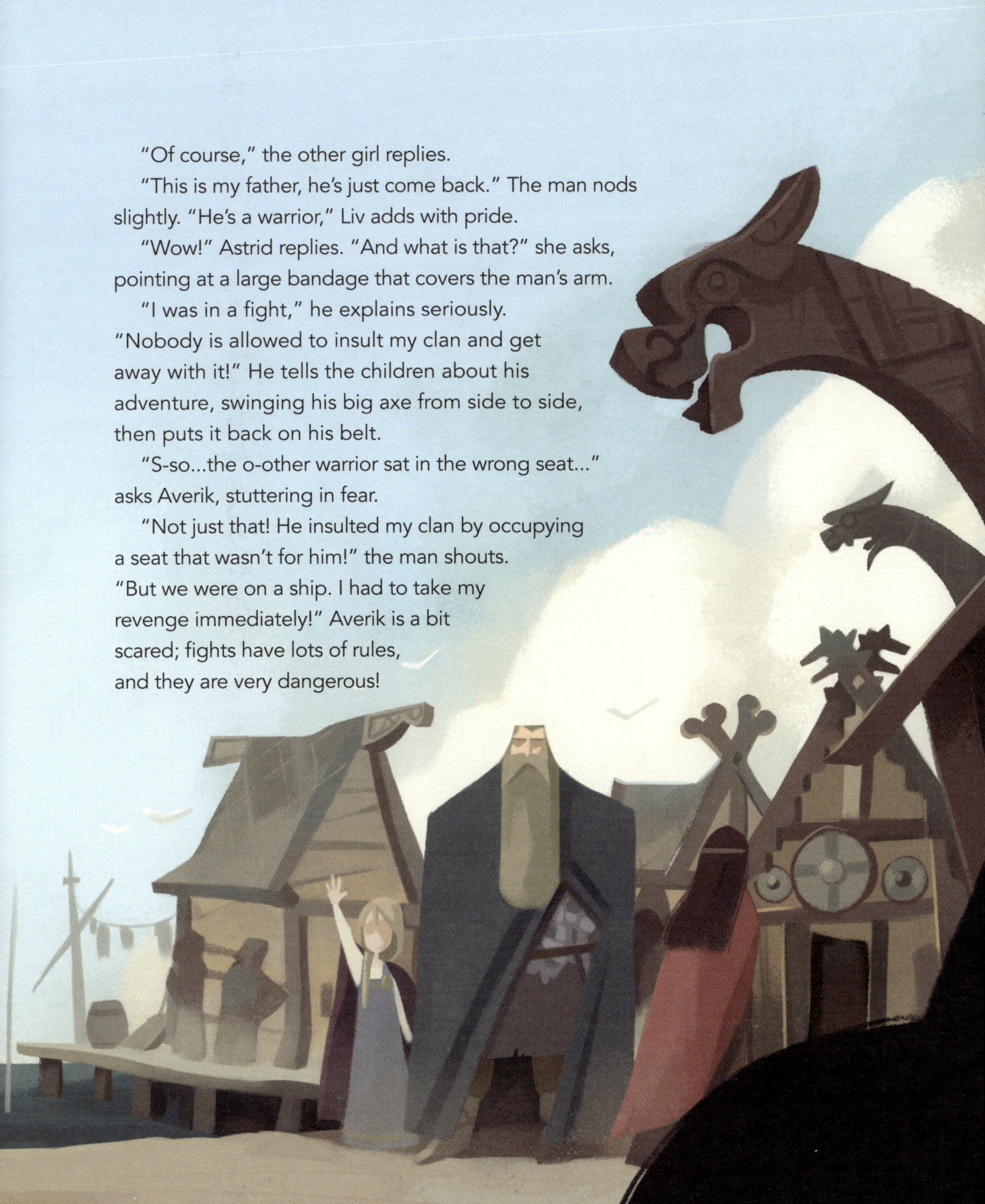

"Of course," the other girl replies.

"This is my father, he's just come back." The man nods slightly. "He's a warrior," Liv adds with pride.

"Wow!" Astrid replies. "And what is that?" she asks, pointing at a large bandage that covers the man's arm.

"I was in a fight," he explains seriously. "Nobody is allowed to insult my clan and get away with it!" He tells the children about his adventure, swinging his big axe from side to side, then puts it back on his belt.

"S-so...the o-other warrior sat in the wrong seat..." asks Averik, stuttering in fear.

"Not just that! He insulted my clan by occupying a seat that wasn't for him!" the man shouts. "But we were on a ship. I had to take my revenge immediately!" Averik is a bit scared; fights have lots of rules, and they are very dangerous!

HONOR AND RESPECT

Hey you! Be careful how you behave!

For a Viking, **honor** is the most important thing. We don't tolerate any type of offense, either directed at one of us or at our clan. That's why revenge is allowed, and there are no limits when it comes to taking it.

We *berserkers*, the warriors, know that very well; we must be ruthless and feared, and each offense must be dealt with immediately without any hesitation toward our adversary.

The god **ODIN** gives us the strength to endure physical strain and pain!

THAT IS WHY WE ARE NEVER AFRAID FOR OUR LIFE.

STRATEGIES

During battles, the most valiant warriors are positioned at the front. The leader is protected by a **trench** made by shielded warriors around him, while those positioned behind throw **rocks**, **arrows**, and **spears** to weaken the enemy. And when the right moment comes, they are ready to attack…with their **axes**!

VALKYRIES

According to **mythology**, the battlefields are roamed by the **beautiful Valkyries**, who are sent down by **Odin** with an important task: **Choose which warriors will live and which ones will die**.
Then the Valkyries escort the souls of the dead warriors to **Valhalla**, the heaven for heroes.

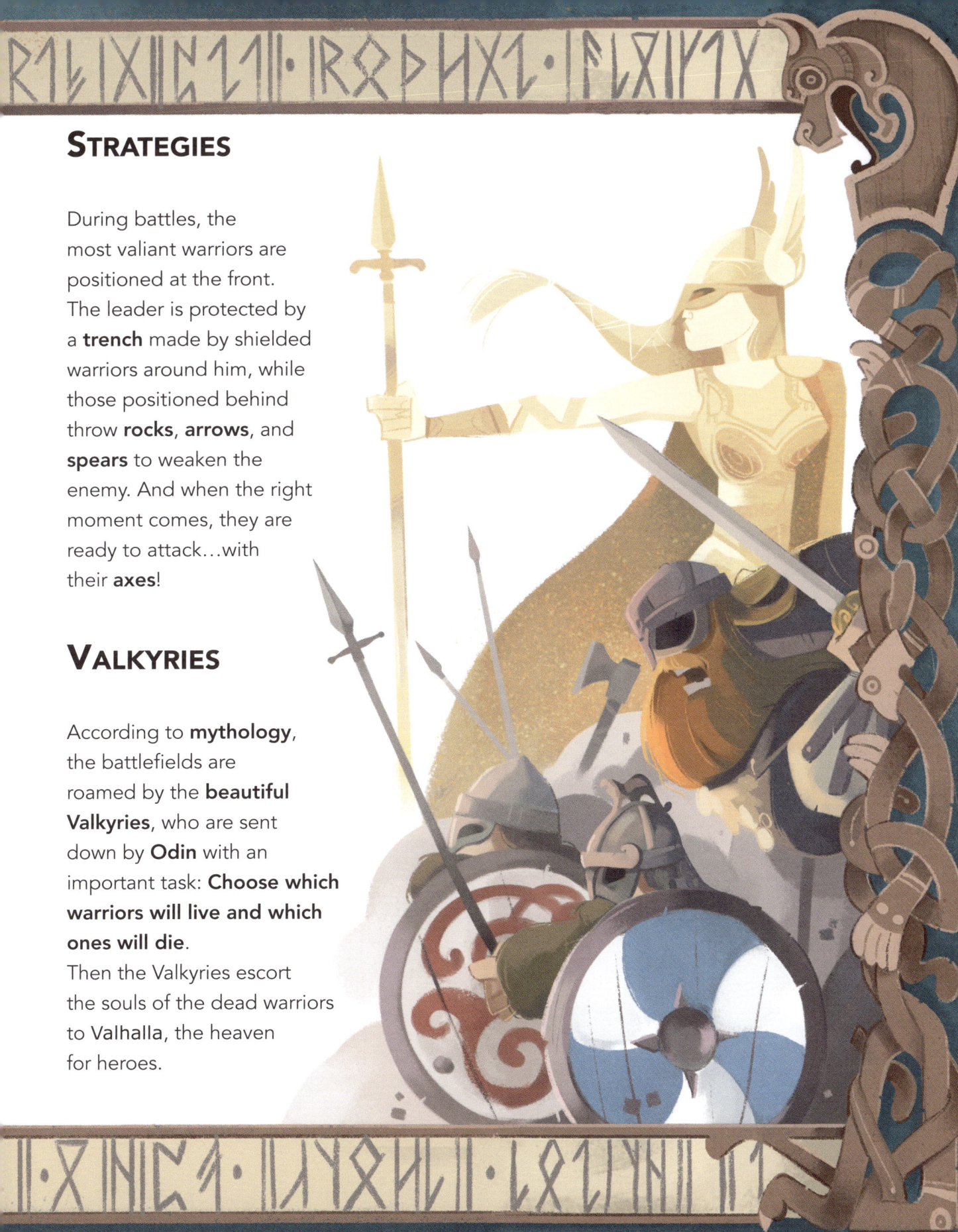

The weapons

We truly are incredible warriors. We have perfected our physical skills, our courage, and our technical abilities in working out fighting strategies. This makes us always ready to defend our honor at all costs!
WITHOUT OUR WEAPONS, HOWEVER, WE ARE LOST.

Let's start with the **axe**. We usually carry it with us at all times, attached to our leather belts. It has a long handle that makes it easy to grab when needed.

Another weapon is the *seax* or *scramasax*, which is a kind of **dagger** with a long, sharp blade.

We also use **bow** and **arrows**, usually before physical combat, in order to strike and reduce the number of enemy warriors.

The **sword** contains a lot of iron; for this reason, it is a weapon mainly carried by the aristocratic military leaders. The sword hilt is decorated with carvings of magical runes, to give valor and power to the warrior.

We also use spears.
There are many different types,
depending on the circumstances.
They can be thrown from a long distance
or used for close combat.

To complete the military equipment, we have a shield and helmet. The shield is round and made of wood so that it's light and the weapons thrown by the enemy get stuck in it without breaking it. The helmet is made of metal, but, remember, **IT DOESN'T HAVE HORNS**, which would be impractical and dangerous during fighting! It is, however, equipped with a nose guard.

Spear

Helmet

Sword

Chapter 4
DISCOVERING REMOTE LANDS

A deep voice startles Averik. "Here you are, finally!"

His uncle is suddenly standing in front of him!

"I'm Ottar," he says, staring at Liv's father. The two men greet each other, and Averik notices something—they are dressed differently! Underneath his large, dark cloak, the warrior wears a worn-out tunic and trousers that gather at the shins. He also wears his axe on his belt, along with his sword. His uncle Ottar wears a tunic, too, but longer and of lighter color, like the trunks of trees. His waist belt is of shiny leather like his footwear, which is tied around the ankles with laces. He also wears fingerless woolen gloves. "You have no idea what I've seen during my journey," Ottar tells the children. "I'm an explorer!"

"So you don't fight?" Liv asks, staring at him with her blue eyes wide open.

Ottar shakes his head. "I do if necessary, but I mainly travel to discover new faraway places."

"Come on, Uncle, tell us a story!" Averik prompts him, anxious to hear about his adventures. And judging by Astrid's face, she can't wait either!

"We reached Jórvík, which is on the other side of the sea, in Northumbria," says the uncle. "If this place looks crowded to you, you should see that one!"

The children listen to Ottar, daydreaming about the foreign place he's describing: warehouses full of goods, and factories that turn bones into needles and combs; wood into bowls, spoons, and furniture; and silver into brooches and pendants. And a lot of leather and clay too.

"Everything is like that over there," his uncle continues while curling his finger around his beard. "There is a lot of land around Jórvík that can be used to cultivate crops and build a settlement. Even trading is easier there because it's much closer to other countries."

Averik is not sure he's understanding correctly.

Sometimes it's difficult for him to imagine places that are more interesting than his family's farm, where he's lived his whole life.

Explorations

Are you ready for new ADVENTURES?

As you might know, life here in the Scandinavian peninsula is hard because it's very cold. However, we Vikings are growing in number! The more we are, the more land we need to live on. We are also surrounded by immense forests, which give us plenty of wood to build new boats. That's not all: The Scandinavian fjords and coves are natural harbors that allow us to sail off and dock easily!

THIS IS THE REASON WHY WE HAVE BECOME SKILLFUL SAILORS AND ADVENTUROUS EXPLORERS.

Summer is the best time to navigate the sea. During winter, waters freeze and sailing becomes a challenge.

EXPANSIONS

The first shores we reached when we sailed outside the borders of Scandinavia were the English ones, followed by the Irish ones; there, we conquered the land and established our first settlements, which one day will become great cities.
Toward the end of the ninth century, the Viking **Flóki Vilgerðarson** sailed off into increasingly freezing waters looking for an island that had previously been discovered by Vikings and that was battered by a particularly bitter winter once he found it. So Flóki named it *Ísland* (Iceland, or **Land of Ice**).

Other Vikings called **Rūs** (which means **red**, probably because of their hair color) explored the Russian rivers with their boats around the middle of the ninth century.

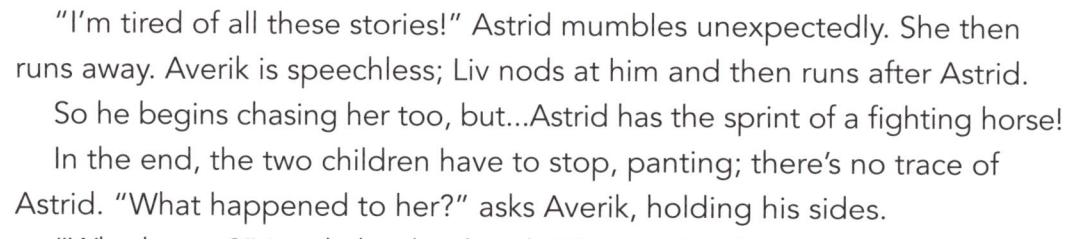

"I'm tired of all these stories!" Astrid mumbles unexpectedly. She then runs away. Averik is speechless; Liv nods at him and then runs after Astrid. So he begins chasing her too, but...Astrid has the sprint of a fighting horse! In the end, the two children have to stop, panting; there's no trace of Astrid. "What happened to her?" asks Averik, holding his sides.

"Who knows?" Liv shakes her head. "But maybe I know where to find her. We need your uncle's help," she adds, her blue eyes sparkling. "Listen to me carefully. Astrid knows everything about ships, and my father was aboard a *snekkja*," she says, pointing at a beautiful ship with a scary-looking head carved into the bow. "She would never get on that one, as she knows how dangerous military trips are."

"Are...are you saying that she got on a ship???"

"Your uncle made a long journey to explore new lands and transport goods, as he's just told us. It was a *knarr*."

Averik is shocked. "Astrid is hiding inside my uncle's ship!" he concludes.

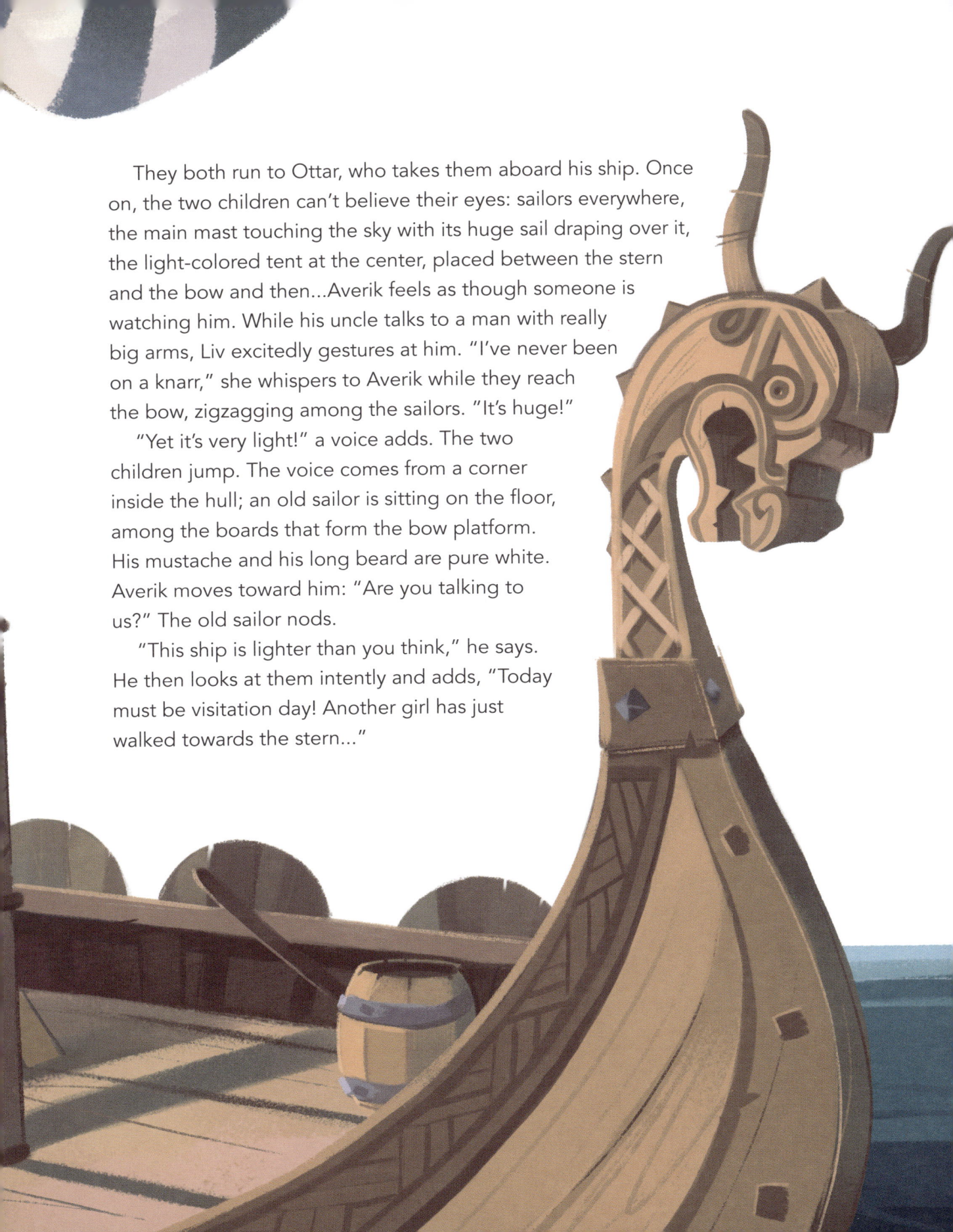

They both run to Ottar, who takes them aboard his ship. Once on, the two children can't believe their eyes: sailors everywhere, the main mast touching the sky with its huge sail draping over it, the light-colored tent at the center, placed between the stern and the bow and then...Averik feels as though someone is watching him. While his uncle talks to a man with really big arms, Liv excitedly gestures at him. "I've never been on a knarr," she whispers to Averik while they reach the bow, zigzagging among the sailors. "It's huge!"

"Yet it's very light!" a voice adds. The two children jump. The voice comes from a corner inside the hull; an old sailor is sitting on the floor, among the boards that form the bow platform. His mustache and his long beard are pure white. Averik moves toward him: "Are you talking to us?" The old sailor nods.

"This ship is lighter than you think," he says. He then looks at them intently and adds, "Today must be visitation day! Another girl has just walked towards the stern..."

Types of ships

Not all ships are made the same! We Vikings sail the sea for two reasons: to explore and make new conquests, and to trade. That's why we have created military ships and long-haul ships.

The *knarr*, which is used for **long journeys** and the transport of goods, has a hull that is large and deep but shorter than that of war ships. It is typically around 52 feet (16 meters) long and 16 feet (5 meters) wide at most.

The *snekkja*, on the other hand, is the most common military boat and is very narrow—up to 55 feet (17 meters) long and 6–9 feet (2–3 meters) wide. It can transport up to 41 men (20 of whom are rowers).

> It's no **JOKE** when it comes to the sea!

Knarr

CHARACTERISTICS OF THE SHIPS

Every ship has a similar structure: bow and stern (i.e., the front and the rear parts) are almost symmetrical, the main mast has a rectangular sail, and the oars reach the water from holes carved out in the hull.

The hull is usually decorated with shields lined up along its border.
The main mast has a small flag on top to indicate the direction of the wind. The long-haul ships are equipped with two small platforms: The one at the stern, called the *lypting*, is usually reserved for the captain, whereas the one at the bow is called the *sax*. Below deck, inside the hold, we keep goods, horses, and cattle that we have bought along or captured during our journeys. The square sail is made of many vertical sheets of fabric sewn together, the *vadhmål*, the same as the tent that is often put up at the center of the ship. All our boats are very light so that they can be moved easily. Their elongated shape also makes them fast and swift, which are necessary qualities, especially for the military boats.

AND TO SCARE OFF ENEMIES, THE BOW IS DECORATED WITH SCULPTURES FEATURING ANIMAL HEADS OR MONSTROUS CREATURES.

Snekkja

Chapter 5

WE ARE BÖNDI!

Averik feels deflated. He and Liv have searched everywhere, even between cases and among the sailors, who were not always happy to see them.

Perhaps Liv was wrong in thinking that Astrid had gone on Averik's uncle's ship, and the old sailor must have got confused. Perhaps their friend is not on this ship after all.

What will they do now? Who knows how many ships are in the harbor...

"I knew it!" Liv shouts, leaning on the hull from the stern platform. "Come out now! We've been looking for you for ages!"

As Averik moves toward her he sees a small head pop out among some sacks.

Astrid!

"Go away or they will find me! You know that my dream is to become a sailor," she says.

"I'm going to stay here," she pouts in her usual style.

Averik has no idea how to convince her. He only knows that they have to go back to his uncle and leave the ship as soon as possible!

"Hey!" a deep voice suddenly rumbles. "What are the three of you doing here?"

Averik stares at the tall man—actually he's a giant—who is looking down on them, his arms folded.

"I'm the captain. Who are you? If you are hiding, then perhaps you are *thrœll*...," he hints.

The captain in person! Averik feels his legs shaking.

"We...we didn't want.....m-my uncle...," he stutters.

Now they are in trouble!

"We are *bòndi*," Liv interrupts, stepping in.

The girl holds the captain's gaze fearlessly, while Astrid reaches the platform next to Averik.

"My father is a well-respected warrior, and if you don't let us go right now, I will ask him to tell everybody at the next *Thing* what is happening here," Liv adds, staring into his eyes.

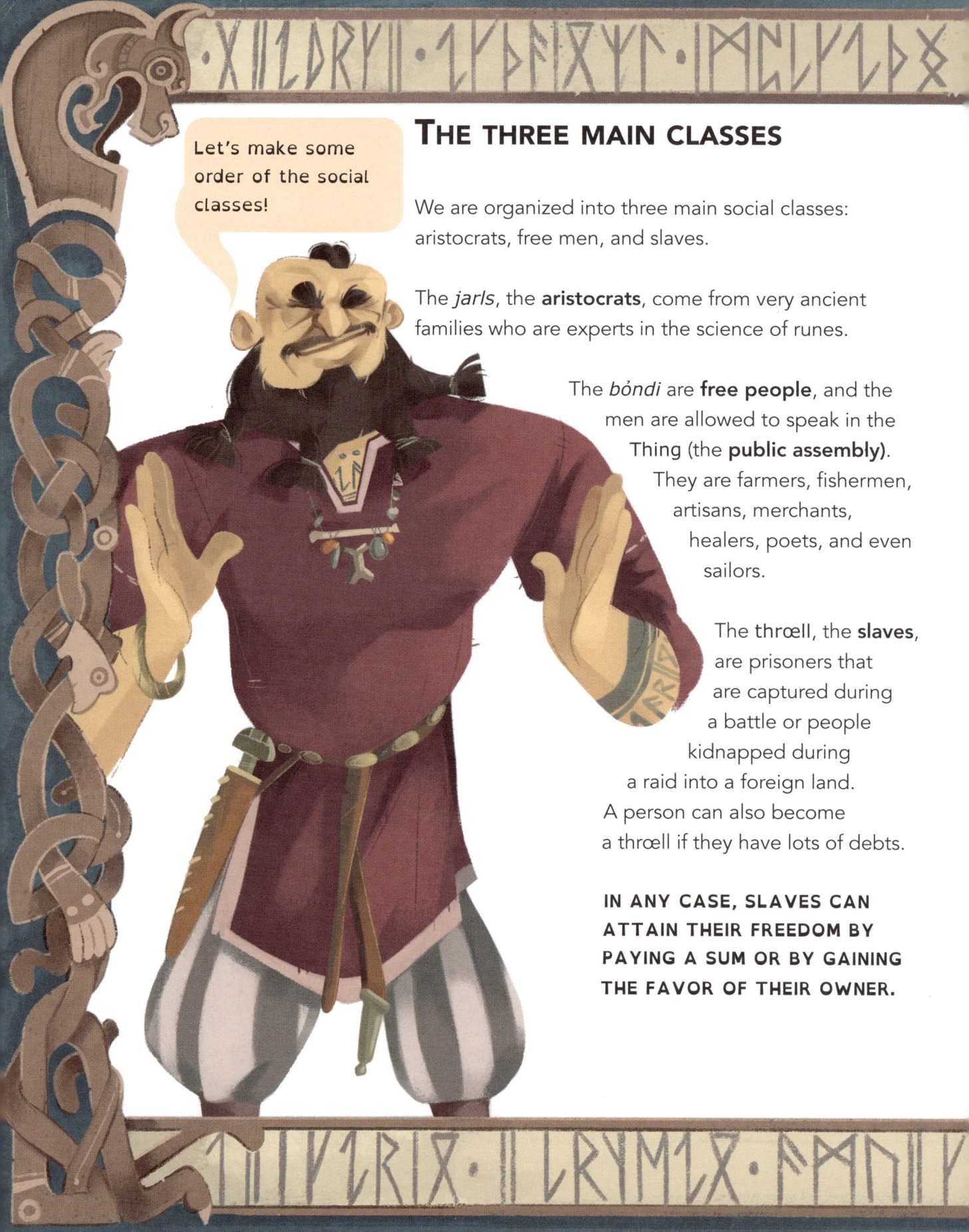

Let's make some order of the social classes!

THE THREE MAIN CLASSES

We are organized into three main social classes: aristocrats, free men, and slaves.

The *jarls*, the **aristocrats**, come from very ancient families who are experts in the science of runes.

The *bòndi* are **free people**, and the men are allowed to speak in the Thing (the **public assembly**). They are farmers, fishermen, artisans, merchants, healers, poets, and even sailors.

The thrœll, the **slaves**, are prisoners that are captured during a battle or people kidnapped during a raid into a foreign land. A person can also become a thrœll if they have lots of debts.

IN ANY CASE, SLAVES CAN ATTAIN THEIR FREEDOM BY PAYING A SUM OR BY GAINING THE FAVOR OF THEIR OWNER.

At the extremes

There is always a **king** as head of a fjord or of a regional district, chosen by the aristocrats. However, the king must behave fairly and honestly; if he is found guilty of serious misconduct, he could lose his power and risk the death penalty. The king doesn't have absolute power when making decisions; he must take the free men's opinions into account!

At the other end of society, there are the *úmagi*, Vikings who are so poor that they can't provide for themselves or their families.

WE ALL TRY TO TAKE CARE OF THEM.

Chapter 6
WE WILL UNITE OUR CLANS!

Eventually the captain escorts the three children off the ship. Phew, no more danger!

Once on land again, Averik hears his uncle's voice—he's not far away.

"What wonderful news!" he's saying.

Averik frowns and approaches him, followed by the girls.

Ottar is talking to a friend of his; the two men are patting each other on the shoulders and speaking with the cheerful tones of people who are very happy.

"We will unite our clans, Finn!" says his uncle as Averik gets close to him. Hearing those words, Liv's and Astrid's moods change completely; they start jumping up and down, clapping their hands! The boy stares at them confused.

"Um...what's going on?" he inquires. Astrid elbows him, giggling. "Another wedding!" she replies excitedly.

Then she resumes her jumping with Liv; they look as though they can't contain their joy. Ottar and Finn exchange amused looks. Everybody is celebrating.

Averik, instead, stands there looking and feeling clueless, like a fish trapped in a net. At the last wedding he went to with his parents, the celebrations lasted days and days...and he was bored the whole time!

The engagement

A wedding is a very important moment. It's the union of two people, but also of two **clans** (family groups).

> The WEDDING is a very serious thing that takes a long time!

The engagement party is called *festaröl*, which means "**engagement beer.**"

YOU MIGHT THINK THIS IS STRANGE, BUT EVERY PARTY TAKES ITS NAME FROM THE BEER THAT WE DRINK DURING IT.

Before getting married, the bride-to-be frees herself from any evil spirit by having a sauna, and only women are allowed to take part. The groom-to-be takes part in the "ceremony of the sword," which marks him becoming an adult.

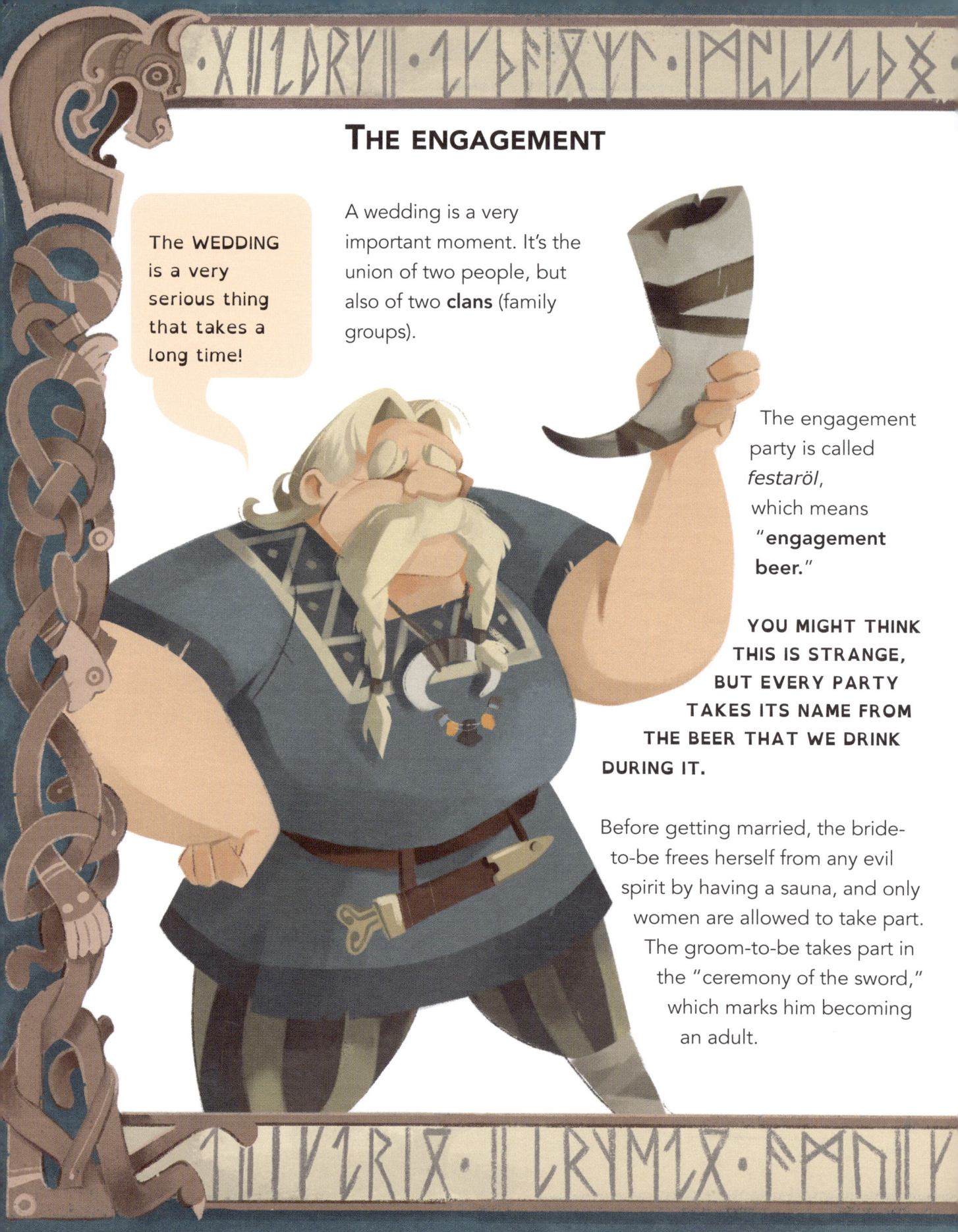

The wedding

The wedding celebrations are called *brůdhlaup*, which means "**the bride's run**." The groom's messengers pick up the bride from her house and take her to her future husband's house! Though her wedding outfit is quite simple, her hairstyle is very important—for the first time, the bride ties her hair at the back of her head, sometimes in a bun.

During the ceremony, they exchange the dowries and make sacrifices to the gods. Then a hammer (sacred to Thȯr) is placed in the wedding bed, as a good wish for many children.
The celebrations can last for several days and involve a lot of guests!

During the reception, the guests eat large quantities of food. They dance, sing, and listen to poem recitals.

Chapter 7

A HARD NUT OF A MERCHANT...

Averik's head feels really heavy. He already knows that the upcoming wedding will exhaust him!

The group—the two men and the three children—leaves the harbor. They are strolling cheerfully when Averik freezes.

"You carry on," he says agitated. "I'll join you later."

He's forgotten the spices for his mom! Without those, he will certainly get into trouble, and the nȧttverdhr will be a disaster...so he better hurry up!

He bolts through the crowd, back toward the harbor. He had seen several merchants there still selling their goods. He stops in front of a wooden cart with huge wheels, where many samples of silk and lots of wax are displayed. "Do you also sell spices?" asks Averik, panting. "Of course, my young friend," the merchant replies with a big smile.

He pulls out a series of tidily bound sachets.

Averik is relieved—once again he's managed to do what he needed to. Now he just needs to negotiate the barter, so he pulls out the piece of colorful vadhmal that his mom had given him. "Oh no, my friend, I'm sorry but I can only give you a handful for that one," the merchant declares, speaking quickly. He's a hard nut to crack! The merchant shows him the various spice sachets and suggests different types of trade. Averik is so confused! It's getting late too. He needs to rejoin his uncle and the others and go back home, but he can't return home empty-handed…so he is about to hand the vadhmal to the merchant, who has almost grabbed it from him, when…

"Wait a minute!" That voice in unmistakeable: Astrid!

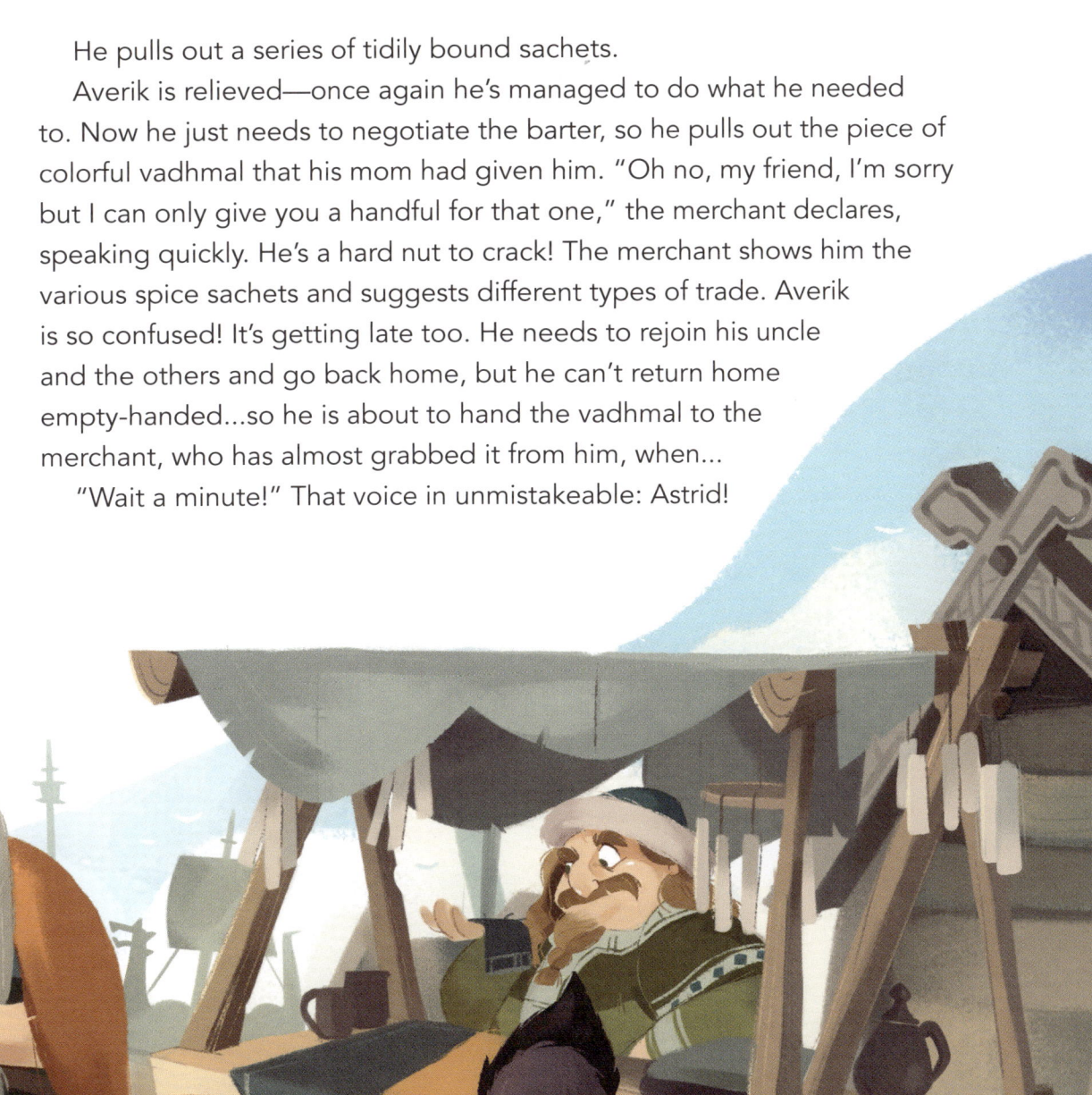

I have the BEST GOODS. What do you have for me?

WHAT WE OFFER

Every Viking is a bit of a merchant! We are always ready to offer something, starting with slaves and animal furs (sable, fox, squirrel, mink, beaver, and ermine that we hunt in Norway and Sweden). But we also offer walrus ivory, greenish steatite (a rock that is particularly good to make utensils), and the **golden amber** that we find on the shores of the Baltic Sea.

WHAT WE LOOK FOR

Anything we don't have we search for during our journeys, such as wheat, tin, honey and silver (that we found in England), wax, and silk and spices from the Far East.

HOW WE TRADE

We usually trade as soon as we get off our boats at the harbor. We put the goods in stalls or inside the same wooden carts that we used to unload them from the boats. **SOMETIMES WE CARRY THEM ON OUR SHOULDERS.**

We often suggest an **exchange of goods** (called barter) or we use coins that are weighed on a scale and given as a payment method.
One of the common barter items is the **vadhmal**, a very resistant fabric that is made with ram's wool.

Averik stares at Astrid in astonishment. She has just made a great barter for the spices! Luckily he still has his mom's vadhmal, so he can finish the deal. The merchant reluctantly hands him a sachet swollen with spices.

"Now go away, I'm busy!" he spits out between his teeth. Then his attention is caught by a woman who has just stopped by his cart, and he turns to her with a smile.

Astrid giggles while juggling the sachet in her hands.

"Thanks for coming to get me on your uncle's

ship," she says to Averik. The two children walk side by side, leaving the harbor.

"My idea was actually crazy," she adds in all seriousness.

Averik shrugs his shoulders. "I don't know about that," he says, "but thanks for your help!" He then grabs the sachet.

She winks at him. "I knew you needed a hand. Without me you just get into trouble!"

That's his unpredictable friend. Her mood has changed once again in a split second...but this time Averik (he doesn't know why) finds himself blushing.

"Come on, you snail!" she teases and starts running.

He has no choice but to chase her again, steering clear of passersby!

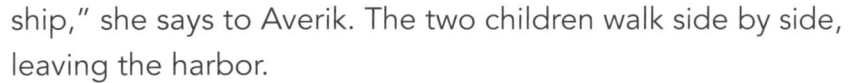

Chapter 8
THE LAST TRIP TO VALHALLA

They are finally heading home! Liv and her father have departed toward their farm, and now Averik and Astrid are dragging their tired feet behind Uncle Ottar.

"What a day," Averik mumbles, rubbing his eyes.

"Hey, hold on a second!" Astrid exclaims "What's happening down there?" she points at a group of people standing in a field.

Suddenly, the whole atmosphere becomes serious.

Averik stops. Strange...as far as he knows it's not assembly time. Maybe something happened.

"These are not things for children," says a man who shows up in front of them. His tunic is worn out, and he looks dirty.

His hands are shaking a bit. "They are carrying the body of our dead leader to his ship," the man says, his eyes filled with tears.

"Oh," Astrid sighs, unable to move.

Averik lifts himself up onto his tiptoes, but the imposing bodies of all those Vikings, one next to the other, don't allow him to see a thing. He spots the shape of what seems to be a boat. It pops up beyond the group of people. Perhaps it's all part of his imagination...maybe. Averik makes a step toward the group, then another...and another... He's almost joined the crowd when a warm hand grabs his arm and squeezes it tight—his uncle's eyes are fixed on him. They are deep. Serious.

He then turns and resumes his walk home, taking Averik with him.

Sooner or later, we all embark on our LAST TRIP...

THE LAST TRIP

When one of our leaders dies, his body needs to make **one last journey out to sea**. That is why it is carefully placed on a boat, along with various things that could be useful in the afterlife, such as jewels and other precious objects.

Then we shoot **flaming arrows** at the boat, which is soaked in fuel, and we let it burn. After, we all take part in the "funeral beer," where we enjoy a series of beer-based drinks. Only at the end of this ritual can the descendants claim their inheritance.

THE SAME RITUAL IS ALSO PERFORMED WHEN SOMEONE WHO WASN'T A LEADER DIES BUT, DEPENDING ON THEIR SOCIAL CLASS, THE OBJECTS THAT ARE PLACED WITH THE BODY IN THE BOAT ARE SMALLER.

Valhalla

In our mythology, the souls of the most valiant warriors are welcomed into **Valhalla**, which is a kind of **heaven**.

Once there, they take part in heroic battles and never-ending banquets with good food and beer, singing and dancing for eternity.

THEY NEVER GET BORED!

Our main divinities

Our most important divinity is **ODIN**, the lord of the sky and the god of wisdom, poetry, war, and victory. Odin knows the secrets of the **runes** and rides an eight-legged horse named **Sleipnir**.

Then we have **THOR**, the god of thunder and storms. Thor is incredibly strong and owns a magic hammer that he uses to protect everybody (including the other gods!) from giants and evil creatures. He also has a belt that doubles his power and a pair of iron gloves.

He travels on a chariot pulled by goats, which he has the power to bring back to life if they ever get killed.

LOKI is a deceitful god, devoted to evil. He generated the **wolf** *Fenrir* (destined to swallow Odin), and he's the father to Miðgarðsormr, the snake that surrounds the world, and Hel, the queen of the dead.

There are another two divinities that are very important to us: **FREYR**, the god of fertility and abundance, and his sister **FREJA**, the goddess of love.

"Come on, hurry up!" says Ottar "They are waiting for us at home!"

He releases his grip on Averik's arm and begins to speed up his walk.

The boy is angry, though. He clenches his fists and, plucking up all of his courage, he replies, "That's not fair, I'm not a baby anymore, I wanted to see..."

Ottar lifts one of his large hands: "You know what?"

His voice is deep and low, and Averik can't help but hold his breath—this time he's gone too far and is about to receive his punishment...but his uncle just shakes his head.

"I don't like thinking about such things. I prefer the god-appeasing rituals!"

Averik's anger vanishes.

"So do you know any?" Astrid interupts. She stares at Ottar attentively, and he nods.

"I've heard about them," he replies. "They are written on the runes."

"I thought only ancient families would pass on the knowledge of runes," she says.

The three of them keep walking, but Astrid doesn't seem ready to give up on the subject.

"Correct, only the jarls can do it," he says, touching his beard. "I wouldn't know where to begin."

"The runes are also used to pass on important information...why don't you keep note of what you find during your explorations too?"

Averik rolls his eyes; Astrid will never change. When she begins with her constant questions, there is no stopping her!

THE RUNES

The runes are **24 symbols** that correspond to the letters of our alphabet, which is very ancient.
This alphabet is passed on only within aristocratic families and is considered very precious, with magical powers.

Our letters are also a bit MAGICAL!

The **runes** are carved with a pointy tool on stones, wood, bone, or any other hard material.

WE USE THEM TO TAKE NOTE OF ANYTHING IMPORTANT, SUCH AS TIPS OF TRADING OR FOR MAGICAL AND GOD-APPEASING RITUALS.

Chapter 9

CELEBRATION IS IN THE AIR!

As soon as Averik opens the door, his mother shows up in front of him.

"Did you remember?" she asks, but he interrupts her by handing her the sachet with the spices.

His mom's big smile makes him forget all about his misadventures!

At that moment, his dad comes in. He's just come back from the fields to welcome Ottar. The two men smile at each other, and Averik immediately feels that the atmosphere has changed.

Celebration is in the air.

Oh no, here we go again! He rolls his eyes...he's so tired after that incredible day that he doesn't even have the strength to sigh.

He already knows that he'll end up getting bored tonight! Luckily, mom has prepared one of her wonderful stews, and there will be so many good things to eat!

Dad likes dancing once he's filled his belly. Averik doesn't.

Mom likes listening to poems being recited. Averik shudders just at the thought of it...

"I'm going," Astrid says on the threshold.

Averik notices that her eyes are tired, too, but she still smiles at him. Hold on!

He frowns. What if...he asked her to stay?

They don't always get along and, unlike him, Astrid is a bit too chatty.

But having a friend next to him would certainly make his evening completely different...

Jacopo Olivieri

Jacopo Olivieri was born in Verona, Italy, in 1966, though he spent part of his childhood in the Ivory Coast. After working as an illustrator, cartoonist, and comic book author in the 1990s, as well as a toy designer and theatre stage and costume designer, in the second decade of the 21st century, he decided to work in children's books as an author, translator, and editor. Today he is published by a number of Italian publishing houses.

Clarissa Corradin

Clarissa Corradin was born in Ivrea, Italy, in 1992. She attended the Academy of Fine Arts in Turin, where she studied painting and illustration. At present she is passionately working on illustrations for children's books. In the last few years she has illustrated several books for White Star Kids.

White Star Kids® is a registered trademark property of White Star s.r.l.

© 2021 White Star s.r.l.
Piazzale Luigi Cadorna, 6
20123 Milan, Italy
www.whitestar.it

Translation: Inga Sempel
Editing: Michele Suchomel-Casey

All rights reserved. No part of this publication may be reproduced, stored in a retrieval system or transmitted in any form or by any means, electronic, mechanical, photocopying, recording or otherwise, without written permission from the publisher.

First printing, November 2021

ISBN 978-88-544-1824-0
1 2 3 4 5 6   25 24 23 22 21

Printed and manufactured in Turkey by Bilnet Printing and Publishing Inc., Umraniye, Istanbul

Graphic layout:
Valentina Figus